FANTASTIC FIREWORKS

*

*

*

*

*

*
*
*

Ba...BOOOOOOOM!

Inspiration on the fly
Published by PoemCatcher Creations
Salisbury Centre
2 Salisbury Road
Edinburgh, EH16 5AB

www.poemcatcher.com

Design by Trevor at Fresh Digital

"FIREWORKS"
ISBN 978-0-9566018-6-5

This book was made between 3pm and 9pm
on Sunday 5th September 2010.
It is full of highly explosive creativity
and should be read with care
(and appreciation)

About the messy bits...

Think, feel, doodle, make a list, ~~scratch some lines out~~, start again, find more paper, talk to your friends, gather ideas, just look around. They are here to be found.

Many of you did,
believed that you could
You did brilliant
I knew that you would
I love your first efforts
With edits and all
The edge of creation
A little bit raw.

P.S. this book is full of mistakes. Such is life.
Some are mine, some are yours.
I don't mind.
The struggle for perfectionism ain't worth the stress.
I far prefer a creative mess.

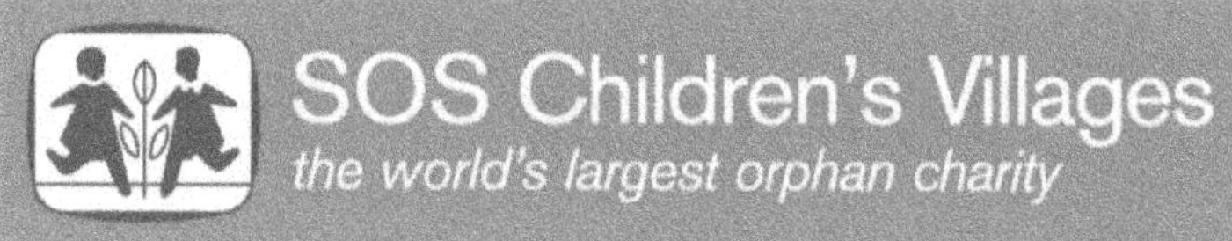

£2 per book goes to charity

SOS Children's Villages provides a family for life for children who have lost their parents through war, famine, disease, natural disaster and poverty. Over 78,000 orphaned and abandoned children are cared for by SOS mothers in clusters of family homes in more than 500 of our unique Children's Villages in 124 countries worldwide. Thousands more children benefit from SOS Children's outreach support which includes education, vocational training, medical care and community development programmes. SOS Children also provides emergency relief in situations of crisis and disaster, and continues to support families in earthquake and tsunami-affected countries.

Registered Charity Number 1069204
www.soschildrensvillages.org.uk

Contents

THE BIG BANG

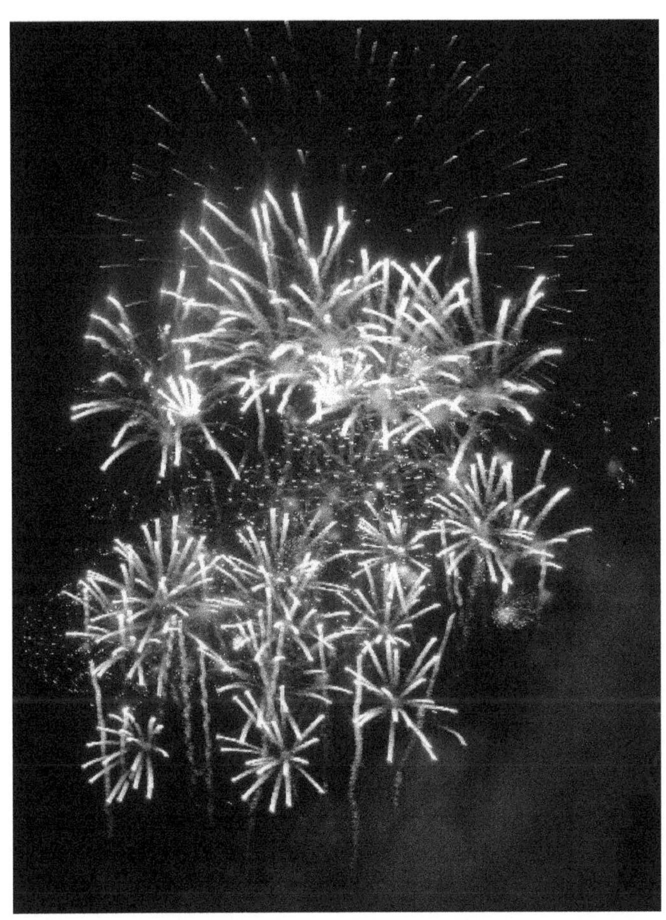

Big Bang

Waiting for the fireworks to start
Breezy night on Castle street
Wondering who I will meet
The PoemCatcher is around

The castle stands so proud,
Waiting for the big bang,
Colours, Sparkles in the night sky
Oh, I cannae wait for the show to begin

By Miss Blossom

Sparkling Light

I looked up, below the castle
Light of fire cascading down
Twinkling waterfalls of light
Falling, falling, falling
Then fading into the expectant sky of night
Wow!, Aaa! Another one!
That was huge!

Like warp speed into the starry heavens
Wonderful fireworks!

By Peter Govan

Sparks

Here we stand its almost dark
Waiting for some shiny sparks
When will they start, I don't quite know
But maybe some will look like snow.

By John Paul

There is no Queen of Scotland

(But I sure do love fireworks)

Dear Queen of Scotland
You don't exist, that's ok
These fireworks Rock!

By Ellen Santa

A Whistle in the land of the thistle

Have had to travel far
To wait in a Scottish Bar

Though in cold
We hope the fireworks are bold

The beauty of the fireworks
Caste an illuminatry glow on Greyfriar's Kirk

Fireworks make a whistle
In the land of the thistle

By Kable Able

The Goat

I’m a goat not a firework.
A firework flashes and that would be
Rude if a goat did.
But a goat can jump over a moat
A firework can as well but only if it’s
On fire
And a goat on fire would be cruel

By Nick Smith

Works become fired
Feet remain tired
Edinburgh get more seats

By James Bertram

My Wife's Love...

Fireworks explode in the night
Like love when a woman's shirt comes off
Thicker that the highest mountains
Filthier than the festival loo
Love explodes like fireworks from me to you

By Chris Wallick

POEM TITLE My wife's breasts

Fireworks explode in the night
like Love when a womans shirt comes off
Thicker than the highest mountains
Filthier than the festival loo
Love explodes like fireworks from me to you

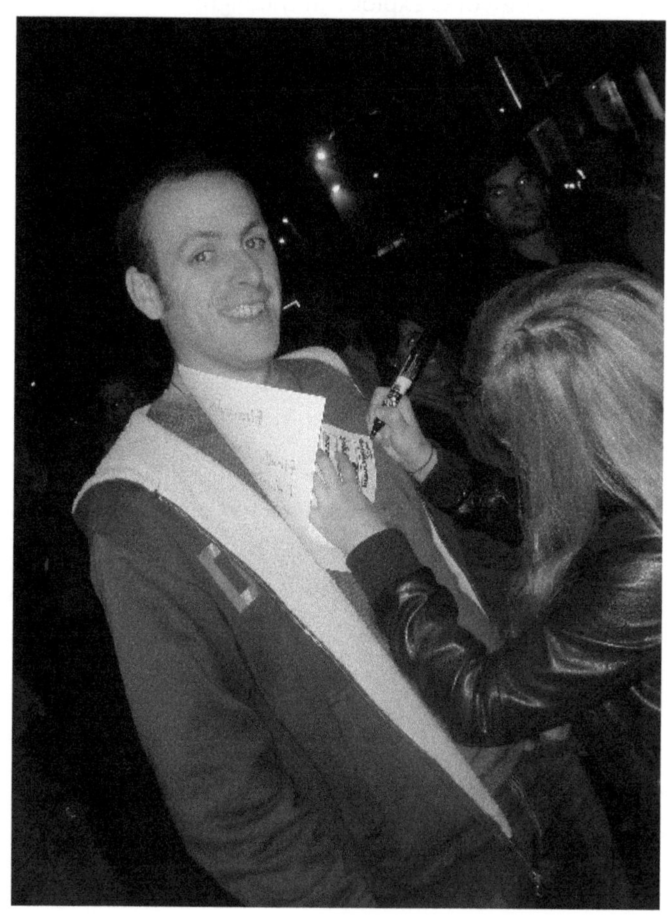

POEM TITLE Fireworks

finally I get to see
fireworks above me
& not on the TV

Lovely!

By K. Angus

BA...BA...BA...BOOM!

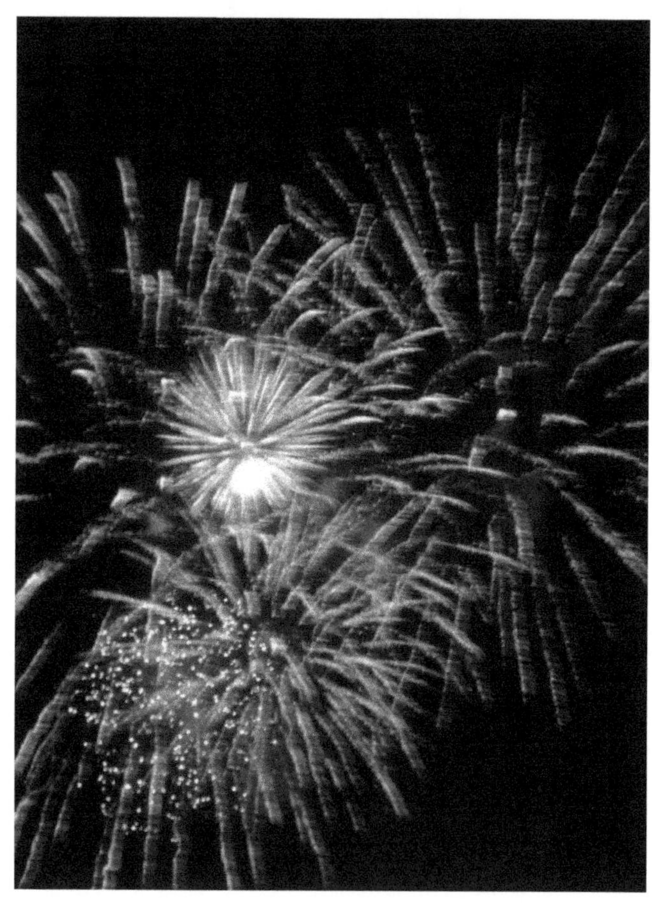

Here there and everywhere
The fireworks light the sky
Blue, red, yellow, pie
Can't wait to see the waterfall
Thanks for the ride

Anonymous

POEM TITLE Boom

Boom!
WHIZZ BANG!
Boom!
WHEE, OOOOH
fountains of light fall on
GOD'S CHOSEN City.
WEEE!
OOOOO!

By Doug Mitchell

TITLE Boom!!.

I See London
I See France
I See Edinburgh's
End of FESTIVAL
FIREWORKS!!!
THEYRE
PANTS!

By Sarah Candlish

KABOOM!

Wham, Bam a boom boom
I'm standing here with a pair o'shrooms
On a cold Edinburgh afternoon
Waiting on the light of the silvery moon
Or to be illuminated by fireworks.

By Smausage

VISITING POETS EXPLODE

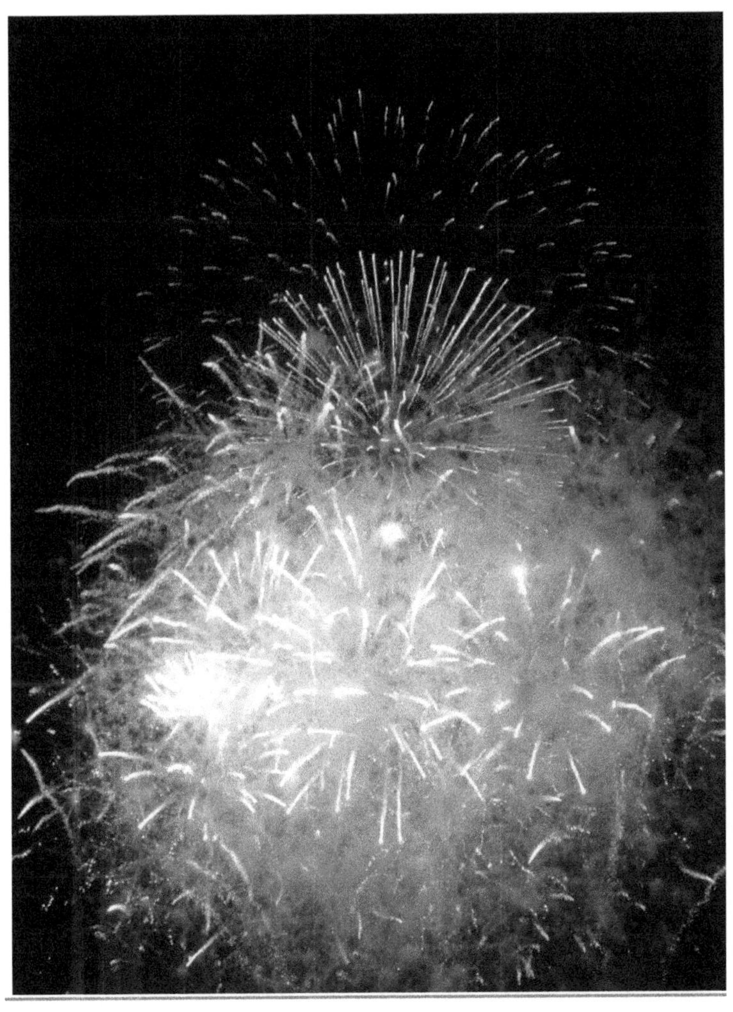

Feuerwerk ist gut
Feuerwerk gibt Mut.
So kommt alle her
Nach Edinburgh nah am Meer.
Everyone here just Move your feet
Who decided to Look the fireworks at Castle Street

By Martin Roth

DONATE A POEM

POEM TITLE LATVIAN STYLE

Bēdu, manu lielu bēdu,
Es par bēdu nebēdāju
Leku bēdu zem akmeņa,
Pāri ejam dziedādamas!

Krista

Fireworks girls from LATVIA

Anne ANNA

By Zannas and Krista

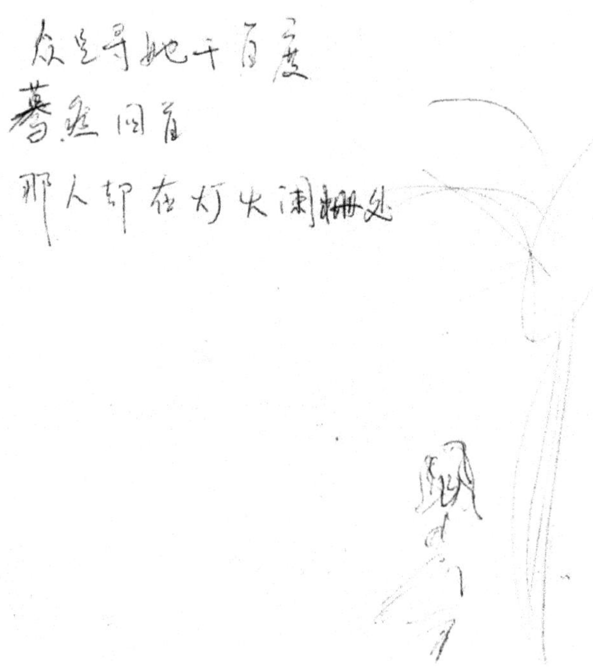

By Yang Zhou

POEM TITLE Suvi suomen

Lopuillaan on suvi suomen
kaikki itkee
Aluillaan on syksy skotiannin
kaikki itkee
Tytöt mininameissaan
kaikki itkee:
FIREWORKS!

By Jenny

DONATE A POEM

POEM TITLE Le dolci Note nel Vento Veneto[?]...

Vola planando su fuochi danzanti...

Trova il tesoro nella singola nota...

e si posa sul castello fatato nella

notte magica....

In questa serata magica in compagnia di
note e magici fuochi dorati e danzanti
i pensieri sereni accompagni.
Note danzanti che si rincorrono nel vento,
suonate e date vita a poetiche
melodie.

By Claudia Santa

Aiming for the stars
Almost reaching them with my hands
I look to the sky
And is looking cold and black
I want to reach the sky
With colours and warmth
Fireworks will be in my way
The feel closer to the stars

By Nelly

Nelly's email is a Yahoo.es address. I'm not sure which country this is, but I'm always specially grateful to those contributors who do not speak English as a 1st language. Well done.

FIREWORKS

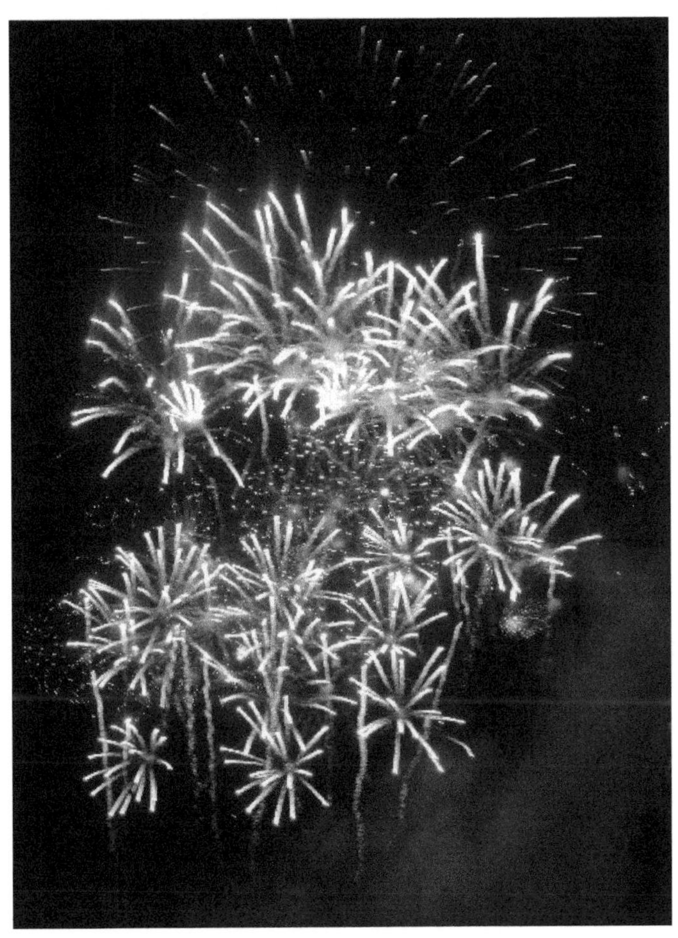

Fireworks

The fireworks are showing at Edinburgh Castle
The crowds and the revelers are being no hassle
It definitely worth it so don't be a jerk
Visit Edinburgh Castle for de final fireworks

By Michelle Murr

DONATE A POEM

POEM TITLE Fireworks, fireworks!

– Fireworks, fireworks!
All a-bang
– Fire Works, fireworks!
Come join the gang
– Fireworks, fireworks!
Lovely bright colours
– Fireworks, fireworks!
Loud above us.

By Carol Purves

Fireworks

Fireworks are great
Fireworks are bright
So we enjoy them
Every night

By Sara Geschonke

DONATE A POEM

POEM TITLE FIREWORKS

FESTIVAL
FIREWORKS
FANTASTIC

Fireworks,
He wanted
Fireworks.

And they came,
Explosive
Magnificent!
Illumination!

Gone
In a flash
What was left?
Silence
Just silence

By Gillian Allen

Work's of fire

The spark in her eyes
Worked on him like
Fire burning in his heart
Creating a work of fire.

Anonymous

Foolish Youth

Foolish youth, life is never what it seems,
The glamour of consumerism, the insatiable dreams
The love, the lost and the broken,
There is no such tragedy
Life is like a firework, you've gotta soar,
Live life to the max, share the world
Every minute, every second,
Just like a firework

- Make sure you're seen.

By Danny Yin

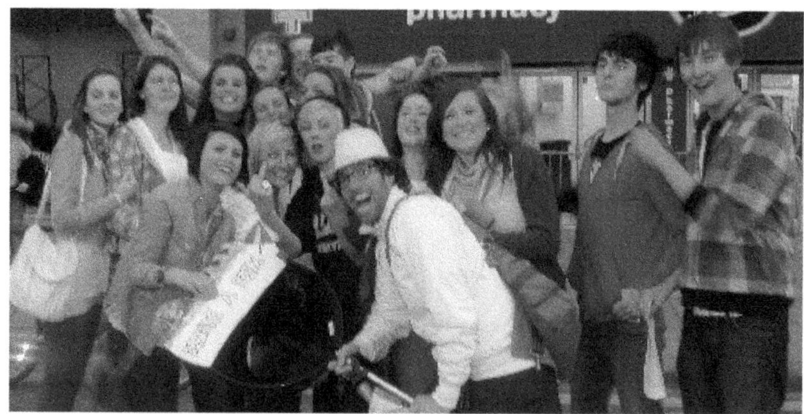

Oooohhh!

Uplit Castle
Floats in dark
Mouths gape open
As the fireworks start

By Dave Berry

A life of colour

The explosion of the birth
Worlds joining worlds
Colour experienced from the inside out
Crystalling matrices like fireworks explode

Once again an opportunity to experience
A life of colour.

By Kathleen Murray

Pyromania on the mound

Fireworks go
Bang
   Sparkle
And something else.
They also go pop
Just like a weasel
Or my dad

By Ben, Richard, Paul and Kay

If wot u felt 'then' was true luv…
Then it's never too late
If it were true luv then
Why wouldn't it be true now?

If I were ever to find true luv
I'd cross oceans for it
& sieve it with both hands –
If I didn't I'd hope one day
I would.

By Shaz69

Sparkling Night

In search of a firework
Here we lurk
The music keeps our feet a tapping
The audience are clapping
Appreciating all that's happening
The 2010 Festival is at an end
Our best wishes to all we send

By M Shields

Women

Fireworks fireworks
Go like a bang
Just like a women
Goes cha cha chang
Then she just can't
Stop like
Snap, crackle and pop

By The Lads

Lights of History

It seems a history runs deep
It is so pure it fills the street
So off I go and on my way
First time in Scotland oh what a day

By Kevin Ford

It was a coal black cozy night
A gentle cool breeze stirred, then
All of a sudden a thunderous
Mighty multocolorored light lit up
The sky with the fireworks radiant
Bright. And the haunted shadows
disappeared out of the night. It
was that scary I had to grab
my toilet roll and go for a quick
shite

By Brian Yardley

This is the type of poem that challenges my editorial vision. Starting with such poetic melancholy and ending, well crappy. I could edit the poem. I could leave it out, but I'm reminded that this is about raw, unpolished creativity, and this poem qualifies, as much as the next.
Thanks Brian. Well done.

Because it is so very long

Fireworks go bang and whizz
They're better than a glass of fizz,
And in this queue we'll get some zizz
Because it is so very long.

Because it is so very long,
We've time to stand and talk and chat;
For sitting in the park I've got a mat,
And 'gainst the cold, a wooly hat

By Ewa Hibbert

Queue

The queue for the fireworks
Is awfully long
Assuming my lyre works
I'll write you a song.
I do hope that the pyre works
And burst into flame
Electrical wireworks
Are likely to blame...
... if it doesn't ignite
In that case tonight
I tell you no fib
Would be a damp squid

By Edward Hibbert

Fiery limbs

Impulses of technology

Red Signals of

Energy Shell levels

By Duguld MacGilp

Limerick 18:24

There was two gals from New York
Who really were an odd kind of sort
They took a look
And stopped on the corner to write a book
The fireworks were the talk of the day

By Amy and Sheri

Amy and Sheri were in Edinburgh for the World Duathalon,
This poem was dictated to me on Cockburn street corner
while eating a baked potato.

Bright Sky

Fireworks light up the sky
They make people come together
And smile
Fireworks are so bright
Sometimes I get a fright
My friend got marries got married on
Fire works night

By Nina Henderson

Abundance

Fireworks in abundance
Look & see, you've one chance
It is a lot of fun, Hans
That Catherine Wheel has spun
Wance.

By Joyce M

In front of us stands a time traveller
To frighten, to entertain, to earn his living
In days past outsiders were not welcome,
Walls were built, battles were fought, alliances made
All to stop their plunder & Pillage
Today, with arms open, we welcome them
For their ideas, for their wealth, for their spirit
Lessons from the time traveller.

By Kumar Gupta

CHILDREN

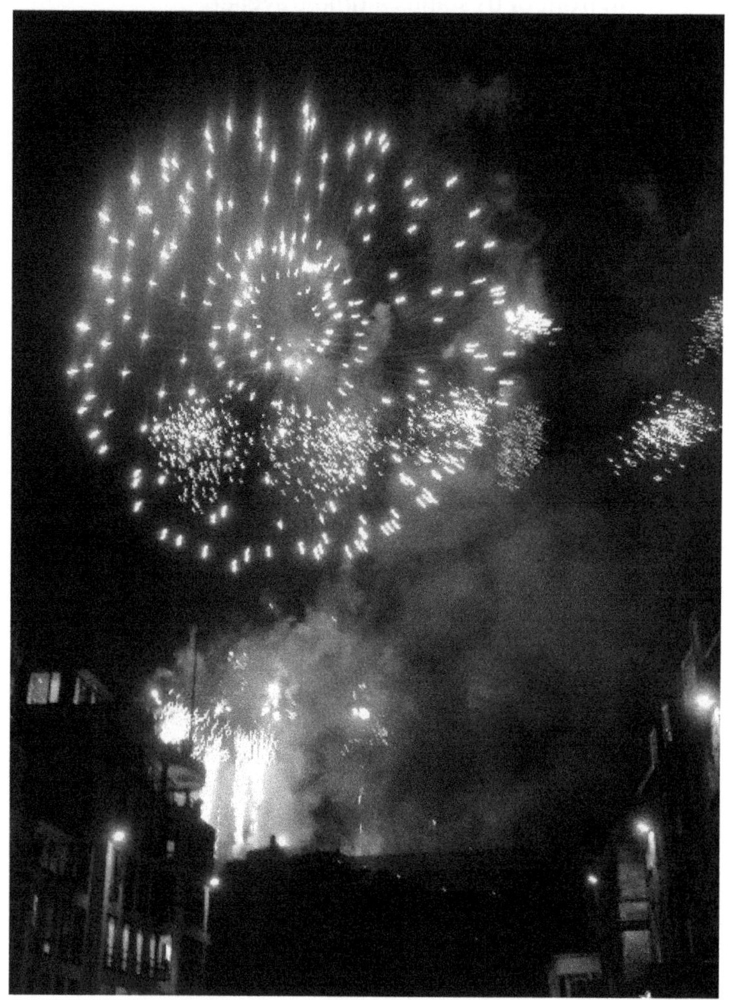

The Awesomeness of Fireworks

A splash of colour bursts through the night
Makes everyone go "Oooh 'n' Ahh"
All the little children giggle with delight
Beautiful & Elaborate cobwebs spread over the sky
To think it was contained in a tube & out with a bang
Makes everyone jump with fright

Fireworks...They are one of those things that
are enjoyed by all

What ever your age
They make you feel childish and silly....and very giddy

By Maria Shah

Children's Cheers

Bang, crash the fireworks sing
Lightly brighting up the sky

Children's hands swaying around
As the sparklers lie down

Smiles and cheers as the all sound
Laughs and screams as the
Children run and hide
Waiting for the bang watching
For the bright colours filling the sky
Bang, crash the fireworks sang

By Erin and Shannon

The Fireworks

"POP" up in the air
BANG
Lots of colours
BANG
Up and then land back down
Once all the colours are gone
Its all smokey
BANG
The big green firework
Lands in the tree

By Ehkoemagbe Brody

TITLE Whoosh

Crash boom bang

Bong. Bang

Whish

f3333 3

pffffh

Wee e

ZZZzzzz

By Eilidh Kemp

WAITING

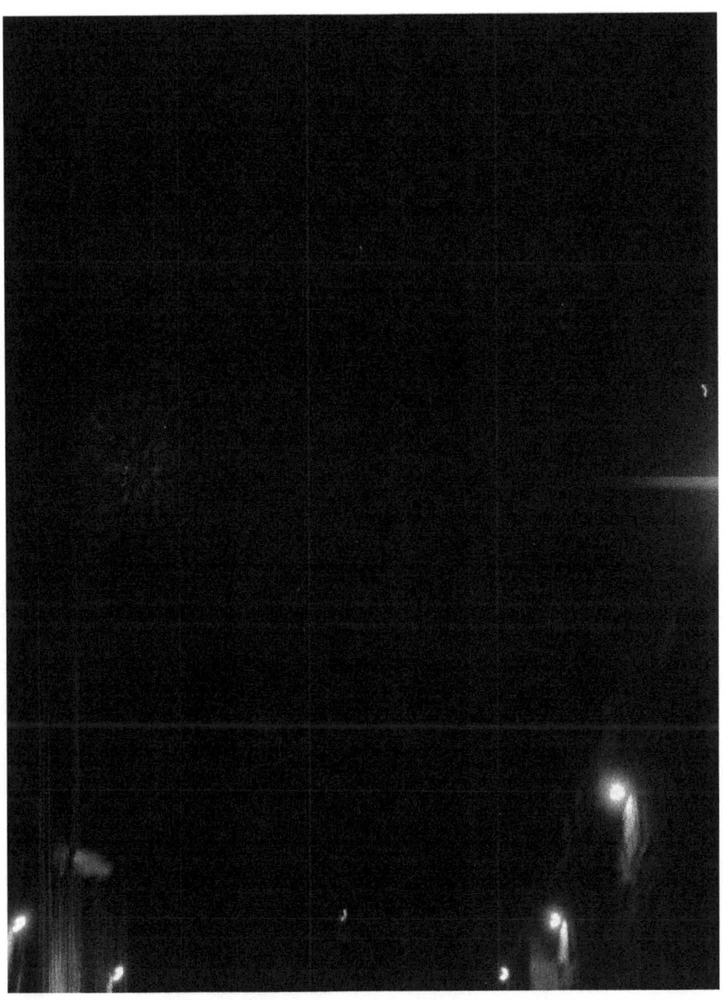

Firework Calls

Medic on a bike
For the festival
Around the city
For the sick and well
Fireworks tonight
To light up the sky
Hope people stay well, coz
Then home I can fly

By Julia Barnes

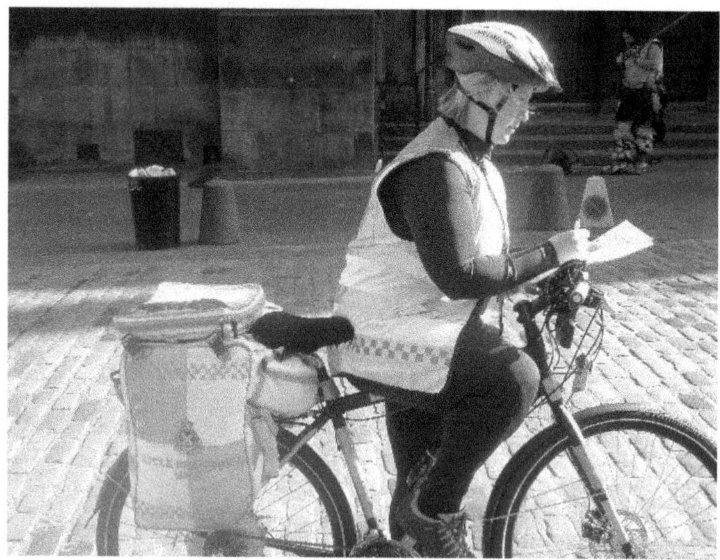

A Lovely Day

The sun shines in the sky
The birds sang, then I caught his eye,
We walked around
To a lovely sound,
Then we sat on the ground
The music played, the fireworks came
As we sat there we were thinking the same,
A lovely day, a lovely nite
Not one bit of badness was in sight,
Then we had one kiss
A kiss I will never forget
And a kiss I will always miss.

By Charlene Durnan

Lost Love

Let the stars shone above my head
I cannot believe the things I said
Let the fireworks redeem my soul
So I once again can be whole.

By Ann Voigt

I missed the festival this year
This made me awfully sad
But the (horrible) kids in paisley more exercise
And my bank balance can't be happier
Viva la P.E. Teachers!

By Sheena

Hi Sheena, I hope the fireworks made up for missing the festival.

Shades of Now

Cold and windy shades of brown
Fireworks crackle, shudder around you now
Black and dreary shades of grey
Blue and purple end of day.

By Hudson

Dave

There once was a firework named Dave
He was certainly not one of the brave
As he was scared of the dark
And so with every spark
He shot away to look for a cave.

By Sheen a Dickson

£5.80 an hour

I would like to see the fireworks
Alas I have to work
For minimum wage
In a job I hate
Instead I will see them through a window
While my boss shouts at me
(FIRE) WORK! ☹

By Carla

POEM TITLE fireworks

Festival
Intense
Really loud
Exitement
Wonderfull.
O ooooo oooo
Really Really loud.
Kaboom!
Silence - its over

By Shryan

The feeling of brushing that hard
Firework against my pal is am
Orgasmic, and adrenalin rush
That makes me feel so alive
A sparkler can make it so
Much fun and the best
Thing about this hot, intense
Activity is I'm rather good with
Matches. My mum says my behavior
reflects my passion. I blame it on the
fireworks.

By Cautney Hazlett

Fabulous

Incendiary

Razzle Dazzle

Eruption

Wonderful

Orchestra

Romantic

Knock Out

Stupendous

By Oliver, Charlotte, Angie and Sara

Firework Fun

Fun Family Fireworks
The end of the summer has come
How lucky we are
    To have Edinburgh...
And each other
    Who cares if there's no Sun!

By Alison Fox

The Catherine Wheel

My Love is like a firework
I can explode at any time

My love is like a Catherine wheel
I'm going round + round + round

When I fizzle out
My spark has surely died.

By Claire MCalloch

As the eve dawned on the city of fireworks
- Gorgeous meal, a Riesling and a fish –
The fireworks will brighten the sky
- Could you grasp the totality of the blue above?
Moments of Joy, moments of Drink, Moments of silence,

Shared for those who care, but mostly for those who don't.

By S.C.A.M.

THE BIG FINISH

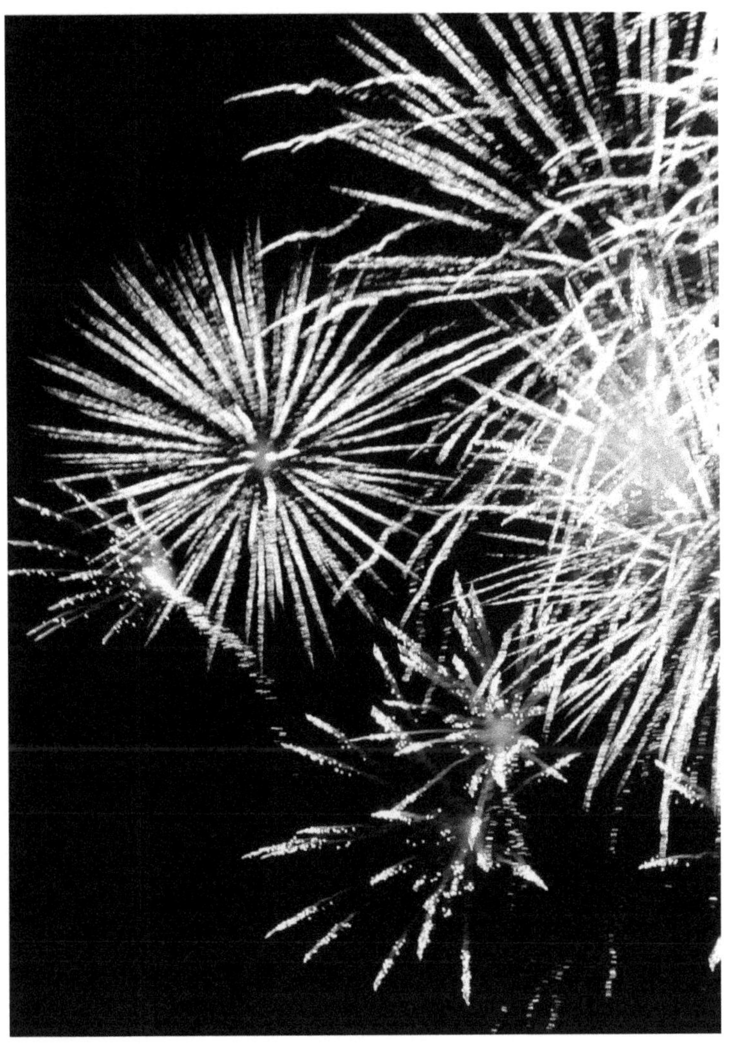

It started on the morning of the 5th of September
We woke up and realized we had something to remember
It wasn't just the fireworks that was on this day!
It was Gillian's birthday
Hip, Hip, Hoooooraaaaaay

By The Bookers

Festival End

Festival night at Edinburgh Castel
Lots of people but no hastle
Fireworks lighting up the sky
Above the castle and way up high

Now the festivals at its end
I'm off home now with my friend
But we'll be back again next year
To have more fun and drink some beer.

By Linda Wilson

Closure

Here in Edinburgh we stand
A night of fireworks we demand
Surrounded by family and friend
As the festival comes to an end.

By Siobhan Lynch and Laura Almond

Afterfest

The Festival's over, The acts have departed
The City's left quiet, I'm left broken-hearted
But though I'm alone now and feeling like shite
There's music and fireworks to light up the night.

By Dai Lowe

What's that bang above yer heid
That flash of light
The buildings shaking beneth yer feet,
The sulperous smell non to sweet
Orchestra driven
Lights in the sky, may just like heaven!
Well the answer to that my friend
Is the end of season,
The annual event,
With sound and light oh so meant,
Drink a dram and wave goodbye,
To a season spent with lights in
The sky.

By Keefe McKie

Hitchcock & Bernstein's soaring scores
Scorch the air as the city roars
Crowds of tourists packed tae the hilt
Salute each other in fleece & kilt
Rebus, Rankine, murkrous crooks
Edinburgh & Scott, Ivanhoe & books
As diamond fireworks sparkle the sky,
I wipe a tear from my windstung eye
As another festival draws to a close
Auld Reekie inspires both poem and prose

By Kerry Black

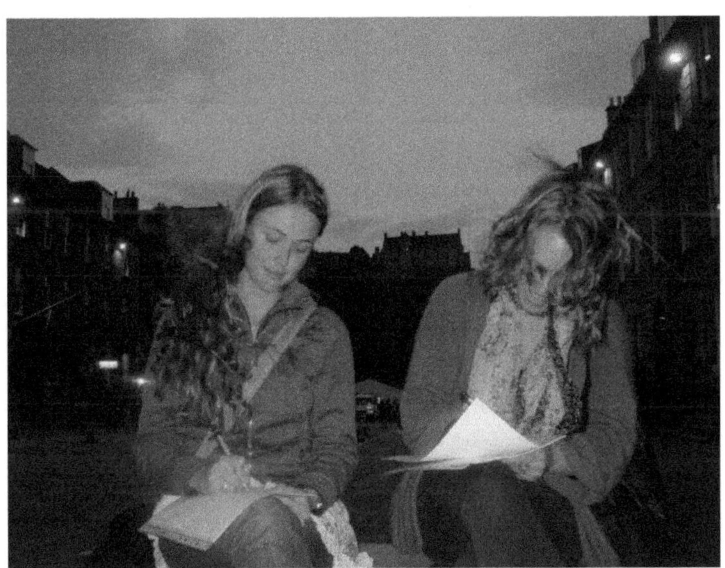

FALAFEL TIME

Falaffeling along

I've got 30 seconds
to write this verse
I must be quick
No line to rehearse
My life is rubbish
In a sea I shall drown
When my only float
Keeps pushing me down

By Sarah Beeden

Jet Fighter

This poem is bad
But I still feel glad
Cause I'm slightly mad
It's a Wednesday night
And this morning I had a fright
As I found a whole falafel
Under my pillow

By Rhiannon Owen

One for the road

I hope you're feeling so super-inspired that you absolutely have to write a poem right now. Go on. Write it on the back page.

P.C.

OTHER POEMCATCHER BOOKS

QUAKE Built from Nothing
Made in 4 days, begging for poems on the pavements of St Andrew's, as an unofficial one-man fringe event for StAnza poetry festival 2010

BALLS from the Queue (Game, Set and Match)
A trilogy of tennis poems captured at Wimbledon 2010 in the infamous queue for centre court tickets.

FUNGUS Poems
Mushroom and fungal poetry written by the world's leading scientists at the 9th international Mycology Conference in Edinburgh

SALTY Poems from the Sea
This book captures the delights of a summer at the sea during the festival season, with rich memories of ice creams, sun, seagulls, waves, golf and all things British. (Donated during "Fringe By the Sea" in North Berwick, Scotland.)

LIST OF POETS

FROM THE POEMCATCHER

Other PoemCatcher Books

QUAKE Built from Nothing
Made in 4 days, begging for poems on the pavements of St Andrew's, as an unofficial one-man fringe event for StAnza poetry festival 2010

BALLS from the Queue (Game, Set and Match)
A trilogy of tennis poems captured at Wimbledon 2010 in the infamous queue for centre court tickets.

FUNGUS Poems
Mushroom and fungal poetry written by the world's leading scientists at the 9th international Mycology Conference in Edinburgh

SALTY Poems from the Sea
Capturing the delights of a British Summer festival in the Seaside town of North Berwick – during "Fringe By The Sea 2010" (This book includes a self-guided historic walking tour)

AVAILABLE FROM
WWW.POEMCATCHER.COM

Would you like the PoemCatcher to make a book in your community / festival / school / wedding / conference? Email inspiration@poemcatcher.com

A personal note about this project

In my therapy practice, I spend time helping people find their vitality; the places in their lives that bring them pleasure and step them towards health.

Creative places are always wrapped in pleasure,
its simply divine.

This poem-catching project has all the ingredients of every dream.

> *The idea; the growing internal detail; the doubt; the fear; the uncertainty; the courage; the trust; the action; the leap of faith; the realisations of the obvious; the moments of sheer stupidity; the 'aha' moments; the perfectly unplanned change of direction; the trashy bits; the lost and found; the success ; the reflection and reward of completion.*

So does each and every poem in this book.

It has been a privilege to watch you write, create and journey through your 'creative ingredients' on a pavement and a park bench.

I have one wish...

Please Believe.
Believe in yourself.
Believe in your creativity. ***Its beautiful.***

Apologies (from you to me)

Dear PoemCatcher

Sorry for the handwriting that you could not read, and sorry for the metric rhythm that you could not follow and sorry for not giving the poem a title, and thank you, so much for giving it a title for me (why didn't you just ask?, I would have done it happily) and I forgive you for typing up the most poignant moment of the poem with the wrong word. (I promise to write neater next time).

Oh, don't worry about the auto-capitalising of all the little-letters I so carefully choose to punctuate. I understand the nuances of word-processing in a hurry.

Lastly sorry for not seeing my own brilliance. I wrote a great poem and then dissed it myself. I've had time to reflect and I'm pretty chuffed that I could write such an amazing poem so spontaneously. I really like my own poem. I was brilliant.

I promise to write some more

With Love
The Aspirational Poet

www.ingramcontent.com/pod-product-compliance
Ingram Content Group UK Ltd.
Pitfield, Milton Keynes, MK11 3LW, UK
UKHW020237250726
13967UKWH00001B/418